PRAISE FOR
*AWAKENING IS NOT FOR THE FAINT OF
HEART*

"The universal journey into the underworld is lightened by being in the company of those whose commitment arises from the ashes of being burned by the sacred fires of what Truth has asked them to bear. Sometimes an outstretched hand from someone who's comfortable with resting in the unknown can give another strength in likewise coming to peace with the abyss. Reading Beth Miller's beautifully poetic book, *Awakening is Not for the Faint of Heart*, provides a hand such as this. Full of hard-earned embodied heart, this book offers both laughter and pain, as well as reflection so honest it almost hurts to witness, and through it all there is a clear stream of awakened consciousness descending to occupy, through love, all of itself." —**Susanne Marie**, Spiritual Teacher & Writer

"This is a very clear book about the dark. Reading this book was like slipping into a pool of presence where I felt myself grow larger and more spacious with each page. In her quiet incisive way, Beth Miller takes the reader on a walk through her psychological and spiritual interior as she is sieged by a physical post-viral illness. It is dark at first. Yet on that walk, with Miller's clear eyes, we are shown a rich, intimate, expansive way through deep discomfort that leads to more room and wonder, for reader and writer. This book shone a light on darkness for me, making it at once more pressing, more personal, more awesome and more intriguing, an effective nudge to

trust one's own darkness just a little bit more. It is an essential read for anyone suffering from their own pain and darkness or the collective one surrounding us all."
—**Dona Tversky, MD MPH**, Stanford Psychiatry & Behavioral Sciences

"For any who believe that Awakening to our true nature will guarantee a life of ease, this book is an important reminder that What is free and ever-present in all of us does not shy away from anything in the wholeness of Being. Life's challenges may include illness, pain, fear and in the case of this author, early childhood trauma, and the experience of Long Covid. Diving courageously into her devotion to "know thyself," this is a story from one whose liberation continually deepened as the fire of truth swept through various levels of both psychological and spiritual darkness to deliver something deeper and unimaginably liberating: LOVE." —**Dorothy S. Hunt**, author of *Ending the Search: From Spiritual Ambition to the Heart of Awareness*, *Only This!* and *Leaves from Moon Mountain.*

"In this wise, poignant, and soulful little book, Beth Miller shares her post-awakening encounter with Long Covid and the subsequent 'dark night' that led to the healing and transformation of deeply buried parts of her psyche, liberating her capacity to love and trust embodied life as it is. A valuable spiritual guidebook for those struggling with chronic illness." —**John Prendergast, Ph.D.**, author of *Your Deepest Ground*, *The Deep Heart*, and *In Touch*

Awakening is Not for the Faint of Heart

ALSO BY BETH MILLER

The Woman's Book of Resilience:
12 Qualities to Cultivate

Waking Up on the Couch: A Chronicle of Letting Go
Death by Death by Death

CHILDREN'S BOOK

A Miller Cousin Mystery

Awakening is Not for the Faint of Heart

RISK EVERYTHING FOR LOVE

Beth Miller, PhD

Epigraph Books
Rhinebeck, New York

Paperback ISBN 9781966293156
eBook ISBN 9781966293163

Library of Congress Control Number 2025909884

Cover design by Ryan Miller
Book design by Colin Rolfe

Epigraph Books
22 East Market Street, Suite 304
Rhinebeck, New York 12572
(845) 876-4861
epigraphpublishing.com

TO LIFE . . . AND HOW IT IS

FOREWORD

In your hands, dear reader, you hold something precious. You must be wanting to wake up or you wouldn't be moved to read this little book. Or maybe you are already there, and yet some of what's happening is turning out to differ from what you'd imagined ahead of time.

Many people in pain of one sort or another—the body kind, the stuff that regular life delivers—are moved toward awakening as a repair mechanism. There's the assumption that if they were awake, they would be relieved, at long last, of all suffering. It is natural to suppose this.

The confusion comes— and often, the profound shock—when they discover that while *mind*-caused pain has been alleviated, in fact Regular Life very much carries on. Which is to say, a person could become quite ill, or fall into otherwise challenging circumstances.

It doesn't feel good to be sick, especially when there is no apparent way to heal. Beth Miller, my dear friend and fellow traveler in the land of What It's Like to Wake Up, came down with an illness that has wracked her, body and soul. Thus did she enter the realm of surrender on a scale that she had not known in the years since coming into radical ease. This experience has become the teacher of them all. She had no spare energy to do otherwise than collapse into the misery, with no seeming relief on the horizon. Bit by bit she learned there was nothing to do but give in. To move *toward* it.

You now are about to enter that land with her.

Somehow (such a revelation!) to the extent that a seeker, or one who's already awake, has the wisdom and humility to relax into the fullness of what the mind cannot sort out or change, this person gradually becomes aware of having landed in the tender arms of the divine.

Enfold yourself now in the wisdom of Beth Miller, who has learned a thing or two about this terrain. Pay attention to each of her observations. You will be glad you did.

— **Jan Frazier**
(Author: *Love Incarnate*)

CHAPTER ONE

I'll share with you the truth I've found:
that life is full of a darkness than can
enlighten you in its own way; there's
a thread there to guide you, but to find
it you'll need to look within yourself.
Meister Eckhart

What does it mean to give yourself fully to Presence—the greater reality of Life. To live your life attuned to and in service of this greater reality; in daily life, in an embodied visceral way? What does it mean to offer what Life is asking of you . . . you specifically.

Many years ago, on a month-long retreat in India, with immense earnestness I prostrated myself at a Hindu altar and engaging my whole heart, mind, body and soul, cried out to God that I gave anything and everything to Presence—the greater reality of Life.

Since that day I have come to learn, in every cell of my being, there is yearning for the truth of what we are, *and* there is embodiment, integration and manifestation in the day in and day out lived life. There is being the truth of what we are.

Being awake is knowing, in the marrow of our bones, in our cells, our true divine nature; knowing, in a fundamental and essential depth of being everyone and everything is connected—animated by the Source of all life. Everyone and everything is a manifestation of the vast, infinite field of energy. Everything lives within and as a field of energy, invisibly permeating and energizing every living thing; an energy that is often experienced as unbounded love, intelligence and clarity. All life . . . water, trees, animals, thorns, humans, weeds. . . live within and as the same Being, and that Being is holy, sacred.

This is the unchanging symphony underlying every one of our lives. And at the same time everything living is a *unique* instrument moving as this universal Presence. Our spectacular world is full of this matchlessness—the distinct quality of the redwood tree, the unique sound of a crow, the silky threads of ears of corn, the gurgling creek spiraling around rocks.

The same is true of the human personality. Deep down we yearn to "be ourselves," to be as authentic and real as our true nature through our intuition and instincts. We long to sing our own song, dance our own dance, and contribute our own signature. It sounds easier than it is; after all the butterfly doesn't appear to work at being a butterfly. It simply is! And yet, look at the transformation it must go through, from being a caterpillar to completely liquifying, before becoming a butterfly. We humans are typically conditioned to follow our tribe, our culture, our family, and our society. In the interest of belonging and mutual harmony, as well as for the sake of safety, security and staying alive, we typically follow along (even rebelling is in reaction to our culture, not coming from the deeper clarity of our own song). We are moved to remain a caterpillar. And something in us knows, sorrowfully, when we are pretending instead of telling or acting our truth.

Not only are we denying ourselves when we pretend, we are out of synch with our calling. Some might call it destiny. Ironically, we are not taking full responsibility for our expression, which leaves us wanting and assuming something needs fixing, when instead the real movement is one of welcoming ourselves as who we truly are. It is exquisite to be fully known and knowing, fully at home with Life and fully animated. It reminds me of coming upon a beautiful daffodil—there is something breath-taking being in the presence of anything or anyone in their fullness. Watching the grace of a hummingbird, seemingly flying in place as it flutters its wings. Nature abounds with fullness. Breathless, beautiful fullness.

It does appear to be a bit more complicated for us humans. We are equipped with a psyche, a word often used to describe the human soul and mind. Psyche as a mental and emotional movement motivates us as humans. In the human realm when we refer to ourselves as I or me, we are referring to our psyche as well as our physical body. Our psyche and our body are constructed for survival—survival of our bodily life and survival of the conditioned patterns and movements of our personality. Conditioning is as good a word as any for the insistent intention to hold onto learned viewpoints and our place in the world at all costs. Awakening to our deeper and true nature requires an emptying out or a thinning out of the many layers of the psyche. It means an abiding devotion to being honest with ourselves, radically honest and radically brave. It means facing our thoughts and behaviors and the impact they are having on ourselves and the rest of the world. Truth be known, we are all wired for self-survival. Every unexamined conditioned thought and behavior is completely self- involved—that is its job. More often than not this fundamental reality (survival at all costs) is deeply covered and buried. For the most part, without conscious awareness and intention, we will be much more interested in how another person is causing us to suffer, or how the circumstances of our lives are problematic and challenging. We externalize over and over, not paying close enough attention to our own thoughts and feelings. When our thoughts or feelings are dark and painful, we are more apt to distance ourselves from our inner world and expend our energy on something or someone out there. In many cases religions have demonized our body, our sensuality, and "negative" thoughts and feelings. In many cases people seeking their true nature through non-duality will, at one time or another, find themselves "bypassing" anything that does not fit the idea of our true nature.

It is also common to internalize our deeply covered and buried darker thoughts. Many of us live with degrees of self-loathing and low esteem. Our dark thoughts look for any convenient vessel or reason to keep themselves relevant and disowned.

It is not uncommon to be more at home with the superficial within and unconsciously feel, in the aftermath of an opening or an awakening, that we are cleaned out or finished. Much is asked of us; actually, all is asked of us. Know thyself is a life-time examination akin to living, nakedly, in a jungle, filled with seen and unseen wild animals. Know thyself is in the service of living and being as our true nature of Thy Will.

In this book I am exploring having Long Covid and its impact on deepening and expanding consciousness and unconditional love. Having Long Covid on top of PTSD from a traumatic background is hard on my nervous system. Being sick for such a long time allowed me to feel into the unconscious belief that I was a victim. An unconscious belief that impacted generations of my ancestors.

Being sick allowed me to bring to light areas of my psyche and body that were deeply buried and waiting for release, freedom, and love. Your portal (spur under *your* saddle) will, undoubtedly, show up *differently*. The deeper message in this book is to make use of whatever pokes you, hits you over the head, or in some way reminds you of your deepest being and to know that whatever is blocking its full revelation is waiting for open arms.

> *Your destiny is the level where you play your tune.*
> *You might not change your instrument but how*
> *well to play is entirely in your hands.*
> **Shams Tabrizi**

DARKNESS

To live as our true selves, our natural state . . . reminds us to be the light, to live as completion, to move as a river flows, and be open, fully open.

While nature simply is all that, we humans are called to a descent into our psyches. We are called to uncover and let go of the constructs and beliefs that block our realization of our true being. We are invited to heal and transform our personal and collective and cultural conditioning.

We are called into the dark. The darkness of the unconscious and the darkness of the unknown.

For this book, I am looking at the darkness we have all experienced; any darkness that has not yet been illuminated by the light of clarity, revelation and knowingness. Darkness as the absence or lack of light. I am not considering darkness as a thing in itself but rather what occurs when there is no illumination and no seeing within that expression of darkness.

Certainly, there is physical darkness, like nighttime or an unlit room or cave.

But for this exploration I am speaking of the darkness we experience when we are confronted with unconscious places within our psyches; the places that more often than not, scare us; places we most frequently do not want to face, much less feel. Given our propensity for survival, we often, understandably, avoid feeling despair, confusion, hopelessness, loneliness, powerlessness, and almost all shapes of vulnerability. When our inner world feels muddled and buried, or tyrannical and overbearing—feelings of depression, grief, and fear will often elicit feelings of being trapped—we look for any distraction. Given our collective religious beliefs, being in the dark can be associated with evil and sin; we might see our inner darkness as immoral or unethical, reinforcing our impulse to look or run away from what is seen as unwelcome.

The deeper context of all the darkness we experience and typically scurry from is the darkness of not knowing (being in the dark). We might be curious about what is around the corner, but for the most part our reactions to uncertainty run from slight anxiety to pure terror.

This is the existential darkness calling us into the profound unknown and unknowing, the mystery and vastness of the universe. Something in us knows we cannot truly know the vastness and mystery we live within and brings us face to face with not being the ultimate captain of our ship. This existential darkness confronts our limited perceptions and ideas and beliefs (how little we really know). It begs the ongoing question about the meaning of our existence, the uncertainties we face about death and ultimately the nature of the reality we are all living within.

CHAPTER TWO

DARKNESS OF THE UNCONSCIOUS

Most of us are very aware of the darkness in our world. Since humankind has been on this planet we have known and lived inside a profound darkness—a profound ignorance of what we truly are. But how many of us look at our own thoughts and feelings and recognize, truly recognize, the impact of not looking and not owning our contribution to this darkness. Unseen, unacknowledged, unconscious thoughts and emotions impact us and the people in our lives daily. Given the truth of our oneness this impact is well beyond our comprehension.

The real rubber of this may hit the road after the initial awakening, when we are called to increasing maturity and willingness to uncover and cop to our pretenses. We are called to genuine humility. As I have experienced the ups and downs of living in this dimension we call the world, it seems to me we are here to grow and to open into greater consciousness of what we are, which naturally leads us to broaden and deepen our capacity for unconditional love.

In fact, it becomes downright uncomfortable whenever we do not express what is real and true. Life asks, over and over again, "show up, show up . . . transparent, vulnerable—naked in the sun." It is an ongoing happening, an ongoing call into manifestation. Life asks us to make conscious use of what shows up in our lives, inner and outer. We are called to understand the chafing of consciousness, calling us to expand and deepen. We are called to say yes to the heart's breaking and opening. We are called to being disillusioned, repeatedly so, as we allow ourselves to BE. We are called to the life-long process of being our true nature, of being whatever we are in each moment, humbly saying yes to serving a greater intelligence, called many different names (Divine, God, Awareness, Truth, Consciousness, Love, Source, Presence).

Being sick with Long Covid for two and a half years has given me opportunity after opportunity to notice and to process a whole new level of embodiment and integration. While it is true that being *stuck* in our personalities can and often does pull the rug out from underneath us, inviting us inward and causing great discomfort, from where I sit, we can and will be brought to our knees at any time before, during and after awakening. Life has a way of upending everything that is not aligned or congruent with our deepest reality.

Almost the entire time I have been ill I intuited something more going on. My body was sick, physically unwell and living with perplexing and relentless symptoms . . . and yet it has seemed to me another dimension was at play here. Something godly about the whole unyielding darkness of physical pain and distress.

To begin with, doesn't it make sense that we are, as pure consciousness, manifesting this consciousness through our bodies and mind? Given that life moves in the direction of greater and greater awareness of truth and love to shine and be unconditionally expressed, it matters what condition the body and mind are in. When we are blocked . . . when we are knotted . . . when we are unaware of our inner life to any degree, it matters. It makes so much sense that an ever-deepening sacred union of Oneness, the seamless unifying of human and God/Spirit, requires us to intentionally and increasingly empty our body-mind vessel of knots, wounds, and gnarly belief systems. A good house cleaning will allow us to sort through whatever is no longer useful, or in need of some sweet and tender attention.

Paying attention to my body is not new to me. Since awakening almost eleven years ago it has been pretty much a main focus. Being aware of my body and physical movement has been fun, like learning a whole new skill and a part of me that I marveled at. This is not uncommon for folks who "left their body" because of trauma.

But being sick dropped me into an entirely new dimension. An unrelenting darkness of not knowing.

And to my ever-growing gratitude and humility, listening attentively to my body—despite being in the dark since there was no treatment available and no way of knowing how long it would last or if I would recover—deepened and activated greater love.

In order to keep on maturing, evolving, healing, and awakening we are called, over and over again, **within**. The commitment to change, transformation and transcendence requires further descents into our inner world. Awakening is a descent; it is an inside job, taking us continually into deeper and deeper waters. Circumstances, although they understandably can take our breath away by how awful they are, rarely if ever, are the stimulus of our disharmony. Our reaction to what has happened is where the real juice lies. The more aware of this we are, the more willing we are to "make use" of what card life has dealt us without resisting, the less we needlessly suffer. The more willing we are to be sincerely and kindly answerable for our thoughts, feelings and actions (the darkness we feel and play out), the more Love can spread itself into every nook and cranny of our being.

The friction for me . . . the call to further transcendence, into deeper love . . . into greater freedom, was being chronically sick in a body that, for most of my life, felt unsafe.

What is it like to be at peace with, to embrace, the body tensions and clenching . . . to compassionately be reoriented from free-floating animal-body anxiety to understanding and support? To become free of vestiges of body-held trauma and clutching?

Long Covid is a neurological virus that, among other things, impacts the nervous system and can wreak havoc on the gut and trigger PTSD. I lived with debilitating fatigue, regardless of how much rest I was able to get and a chronically painful and messed up gut that often woke me up in the middle of the night.

What a perfect storm for facing my traumatized body in a different way, revealing all those wordless places and cells and blood and bones that held the trauma . . . so much deeper than I could touch before. The more hidden the burial, the trickier to uncover and the more powerful to see what it reveals.

It is the facing . . . it is the conscious living in the dark of not knowing until our inner light reveals the truth that is breathtaking. This is when actual transformation can happen.

As I continued to live with Long Covid, there appeared to be a foot-on-the-ground deepening happening—the sacred union between matter and spirit, the deepening creation of being human and being divine powerfully strengthened.

There is the human dimension. One of the fallouts of a traumatized nervous system that is often tense and clenched is not being able to be clear about what the body needs. More often than not, the first thought or response is a catastrophic one that both originates from PTSD **and** enhances the fogginess of PTSD. Something awful is happening or about to happen. And "I" have no idea what to do about it. As traumatized humans we are time and again trained to be powerless or paralyzed, which is why we often don't know how to take care of ourselves in a real, present, and healthy way.

What allows us the courage and faith to keep looking inward when there is no orientation or understanding and we are just blindly going towards the dark? Awareness . . . Love . . . watches and holds all of this. Since there is no real separation between our small selves and our Divine Selves, awareness sees, touches, and knows the full state of trauma. Love is untroubled and untouched by the unhealthy anguished body and mind, in fact, appears to grow in magnitude in the face of true openness and honest inquiry.

This tender and wise holding opens into enormous clarity. It quiets the mind, focuses attention on sensations. Being aware of the sensations, pain and discomfort in the body directly, without any interference from the mind, or history, or PTSD, tells you what is needed in that moment. Where is the pain; what would either soothe or eliminate the discomfort; what support or help do I need to benefit the situation? And often sitting in silence and simply being with the sensation can be just the ticket. This clarity, when not known before, appears simple and yet it speaks to the extraordinary experience of increased consciousness and love.

Throughout my life I have not had a lot of patience. I suspect anxiety was underneath, but I have been mostly aware of feeling inpatient for both petty and major "inconveniences." Patience is key to health when you are physically ill. It was something I needed to actively cultivate as my body ceased to cooperate. Since I was sick, I was pushed to practice the missing art of waiting and seeing; my previously known way of life was now on hold. I had no choice but to slow down to meet the rhythms of my body. I slowed and slowed, watching my orchids bloom and die off, and then bloom again. I slowed and slowed and became newly familiar with every piece of furniture and artwork in my apartment. I slowed and slowed, watching the cars and the clouds go by and becoming a witness to the family across the street go through a divorce. And as I slowed and slowed, I could become aware of deep anxieties and fears; anxieties and fears that were not available to me while I was healthy could finally catch up and reveal themselves to me. Now, at my lowest, it felt as if they were swarming and feasting over me.

I discovered that sickness ravished me spiritually and stripped me to the bone.

Many a moment I felt forsaken. Some part of me was holding onto a belief that being awakened to true nature would protect me from such ravishing.

Having a shelf life and knowing I would one day die became even **more** intimately apparent. It is uncanny to me how true "knowing" of something

(I will surely die one day) can and does reveal itself in layers and layers of instinctive ahas!

It is only in retrospect that I see this time as a profound revealing of a transcendence beyond darkness and light. A sincere immersion into the illusory dark, which by its very nature is profoundly unknown and therefore inexplicable.

Throughout the illness I had four dreams and a vision that helped guide me. The first dream came about a year into being sick. The night before this dream, I was at my wits' end, even thinking it would be preferable to not live, imagining a life of no relief, day after day and night after night.

In the dream I am driving. I believe it is early morning and I am just starting out the day. I am surprised and very taken by the fact that the whole world appears to be gray. The trees, the sky, the road, the bushes, and shrubs at the side of the road. It is as if a fog has descended and covered the entire world— there is a certain softness and beauty to it. It feels serene. I am doubly taken by a profusion of yellow daffodils blooming from the trees and along the side of the road. Hundreds of them, heads down, as if bowing. The yellow is vivid. A technicolor that has through the years gotten my attention in dreams, as if to say, pay closer attention here, revealing something profoundly alive. The beauty and the brightness and the stark substance of them in contrast to the gray of everything else.

What is being asked when I feel so badly? Big

question . . . I could see it was time for reflecting, time to stand back and see a larger picture or perspective.

Two weeks before this, just as I was falling asleep, a vision of the color black seeps underneath my eyelids. It is as if someone has gently spilled black India ink and it is spreading. I am "told" to open my eyes. When I close them again, the black seeps even further underneath my eyelids, almost covering the entire orb. I am once again "told" to open my eyes (in order to stop the spread). The black is serene and very peaceful. Soft as well.

I am reminded of this in the above dream. The foggy gray of the world had the same quality as the black ink—deeply soft and peaceful. Unlike the fogginess of PTSD.

This has been a cellular learning curve of trust. Trust of life, trust of benign goodness, trust of love. If we have not known trust as a baby or young child, we have ample opportunities to repair that as adults. We learn trust by going through the fire with an open heart (an open heart is open to everything, including distress, despair and resistance). Each time love comes through everything in us sits up and takes notice, layering the foundation for a deeper trust. It is not something we can learn conceptually, which is why I bow to all our brave melting into oneness—the sacred union with all of life, in which we are present with whatever shows up from moment to moment.

It is easy enough to trust life when we feel good and our outer circumstances are calm enough that life flows. It is another thing altogether to trust life when we feel muddled or scared and cannot see a way out. It is another thing to trust life when the world appears to be overcome with darkness. And so, in a rich and powerful moment-to-moment presence I became more and more intimate with the dark.

Think of the moist, dark and rich soil that holds and protects seedlings. Think of the darkness of the uterus, nourishing and containing the embryo as it grows to full term. Think of the darkness of sleep— the quiet, alive space we cocoon in for deep rest. Think of the vast darkness of anesthesia that appears to blanket every bit of consciousness.

I recently watched a video with a beautiful and wise man, in which he explains how trees have to grow in two directions at the same time. First, in order to root, the tree grows away from light, towards and into the nutrients in the soil. It must grow down before it grows up. As the seed grows underground, where it is dark and damp, the root system hits resistance. It must push down through the earth to go further. This rooting under the ground, through the dark, rich soil, can only be navigated by feel since it is too dark to "see" clearly.

Once it breaks up through the earth there is no more resistance. The part of the tree above earth grows towards light. It is what is visible for all to see and stand in awe of.

It is the work we do in the dark, when it is difficult and damp that makes the work that everyone sees in the light visible and sought after. Like the trees, who, for the most part, continually deepen and broaden roots, we are called to descend *and* ascend.

Whenever we allow ourselves to be emptied of anything that is distorting our true nature, whenever we follow the impulse to surrender and let go of an illusory identity for the love of Source, for what is most Real, we are more deeply melting into Life and the Self. We are opening and ascending into unconditional Love. This can be the most priceless gift we have to give, the gift of surrender to something greater than ourselves. And then, lo and behold, that which we seek is seeking us. That very same Love we have given our all to will fill our Being over and over and over again. This is a dance we are called to. This is what the mystics have called a sacred union—the integration of our humanity and divinity, expressed uniquely through each of us. This is a whole-hearted praise to being alive. To being alive on sacred ground.

As I look back on the early parts of being sick and the messages in the dream and the inky blackness, I am struck by how dark the period was. There were so many moments and days and weeks that I was overcome by feeling miserable and often sensed a futility. I can see now that the gray fog that was so serene, the black ink that was peaceful was offering comfort in this dark night of my soul. It brought comfort and the message: keep your eyes open! I *knew* Spirit as pure Light. The deep void of complete disorientation and that feeling of being lost in the wilderness with no flash points of light is the apparent **absence** of Light. But this knowing has no end, and each layer revealed is stunning. Each layer burrows us deeper and deeper into the flesh and blood of naked, open-ended, true reality, beyond any points of reference.

I felt in the midst of what Carl Jung called the "dark side of God," the mystery of not knowing. There was no light, and it could only be by experiencing and living through it that I was going to build up more trust in that true peace—that all is well no matter what. I slipped in and out of anything that resembled a larger perspective, but I stayed completely present with every state of being I went through. And here's the paradox and irony: while I experienced feeling cut off from a lifeline I, without willfulness or exertion or effort, was completely present to everything. I was aware of being overwhelmed and miserable. I was aware of how much my body hurt, and I was aware of wanting to be anywhere but here and now.

And yet, even throughout the darkness, I could sense an increasing consciousness happening despite (or perhaps *because of*) the obstacles and relentless challenges.

On a painter's palette, when black and white are mixed, we get the color gray. There is the well-known experience of gray being foggy and open to interpretation, as when we say "the results of the tests were gray," or "we have entered a gray zone." And then, there is the field of gray that appears when the dark and the light are in equal balance. It is one thing to love the truth when we are experiencing the joy of anything that is light, when we feel the ecstasy of bliss. I think it is one of the reasons some folks get stuck in the transcendent state that often shows up in the early stages of awakening. Who in their right mind (conditioned mind) would leave such a state? It is so easy to misunderstand that this sense of peace and well-being is not stable. It is merely the *opening*, the wide door of connecting to our true nature. It is not a final resting place. It is a holy knowing that is an invitation to go further, go deeper; not to be lulled into any belief that this is the end.

Perhaps gray is a state of transcendence. Carl Jung posited that transcendence often requires the opposites to be pulled far into extreme and challenging positions. To go beyond, means experiencing the extremes of dark and the light. Sacred ground is the visceral yes to loving (and being) all the opposites: dark/light, black/white, me/you, inside/outside, up/down, good/bad, human/divinity. Sacred ground is the field beyond what we, in this world of duality, see as opposites.

I have come to see this integration requires enormous trust in Life—no matter how much we intellectually understand that living an awake life is one of being at peace with all there is. In order to truly integrate our humanity with the infinite, we are faced with truly knowing and loving every single part of ourselves, which includes aspects we shudder and cringe at. Trust Life? Given our common human experience of betrayals and hurt, given the daily global reminders of how we tragically harm ourselves and one another, this can be a tall order.

Mystics have long taught the importance of self-awareness ("know thyself") as a pre-requisite to the mystical union of Self and self. And here is the heart of the matter: to be fully one, to be fully real and authentic means knowing thyself again and again. It means facing the dark regions in our psyches, moving through resistance; it means embracing how we have inflicted hurt and pain; it means embracing the wounds that were unbearable to face when they happened; it means turning to face the wild tiger we have run from until we are able to look it straight in the eye.

Fortunately for those of us alive now, we have the benefit of psychology, giving us tools.

CHAPTER THREE

M any years ago, I saw a documentary about Hitler's life, his time in power and his death. It came to me that what we often call evil can be seen in another light. When our mind's sickness and distortions (not being loved or cared for in a healthy way) are cast out so as not to feel our own excruciating pain, we blame someone or something else. This is called projection in psychology. We see the darkness out there (*othering* some segment of humanity, the environment and the unknown) and both hate and fear what appears to be too excruciating to go toward inside ourselves. This results in free-floating, dangerous, and thick darkness. When we are sensitive enough, we can even feel the heaviness of such pitch-black darkness in the atmosphere, both close up and far away.

The dynamic of casting out our own darkness happens all the time. The unconscious and destructive act of projecting is true for all of us. The more unaware we are of our thoughts, feelings, and inner conflicts, the more they remain unconscious and are played out in thousands of ways (including turning it all towards ourselves, which can show up as self-destruction and self-criticism). The more critical and judgmental we are about our inner life, the closer we come to adding to the darkness.

The projection of personal torments is its own flavor of darkness and we have lived with war, inequality and suffering for as long as we have had history. There is a great deal of understanding in the spiritual world that our minds cannot have access to our deepest reality, and that our minds are geared to our human survival and therefore often get in the way of awakening. What does it look like then to be kindly responsible for our inner life? Having taken "know thyself" to heart and having studied psychology for decades and worked with hundreds of folks over the years, I know that the mind holds layers and layers of misunderstandings and conditioned patterns. More often than not we are afraid of the unconscious and will run like hell from anything we consider "negative" about ourselves, so terrified of tarnishing the self-image we hold that we remain unconscious of anything that would jeopardize our veneer. We are typically convinced that whatever is buried in the unconscious is threatening and possibly dangerous.

We can be so tied to our conscious identity that even if the unconscious is sheltering *goodness and strength*, we will not want to upset any apple carts by allowing this revelation into the light of day.

Know thyself, a deeply spiritual pointer, is an invitation into the dark recesses of our psyche (soul, body, mind). It truly doesn't matter what is happening in the "outside" world in a spiritual life. Or to put it another way, it is when we are radically honest with ourselves that we become less and less reactive, begin to see the world and ourselves more and more clearly and will have a benign and loving impact on others. To become aware and fully accountable for our thoughts, recognizing the power and impact our thoughts have on ourselves and the collective energy field, is a hard and important preoccupation. To take good hard looks at ourselves, layer upon layer of thoughts and thought patterns, is an arduous, unending task.

As counter-intuitive as it sounds, vulnerability is always the right choice. Remaining open-hearted and soft in the challenging world of duality is the tee-ter-totter balance we are designed for—harmony of wholeness, our birth-right. We can learn to be kinder and warmer to ourselves, especially to the most desperate parts of ourselves. We are actually starving for this all-out acceptance. We hunger to know ourselves as love, and somewhere we intuit the immediate connection between that warm embrace of all we are to naturally being kinder and welcoming to each other.

CHAPTER FOUR

I found myself in a paradoxical state of listening to my body, narrowing my entire focus to my body's needs and pain, while, in the background, I was aware of kernels of spiritual expansion tapping me on the shoulder or murmuring in my depths.

When we are open and devoted to listening, Life presents us with whispers and loud sounds.

A very dear friend and her adult daughter were at a major park, filled with rides and hundreds of people. After a tumultuous roller coaster ride, my friend began to feel ill—ill enough to know she needed to lie down. She and her daughter found a bench and sat down. My friend put her head in her daughter's lap, and they stayed there for an hour until she felt well enough to walk to the car.

The reason my friend shared this story was to tell me about her experience riding a roller coaster, which she has loved since childhood. While I registered her pleasure, what really got my attention was a deeper discomfort in me. One that let me know, under no circumstances could I imagine putting my head in someone's lap when I felt unwell and therefore inescapably vulnerable.

Taking that to heart, I let my resistance sit and breathe.

Yes, I was living in a very spent body—at this point, fourteen months of not being well—and, yes, I was living with daily symptoms of a messed-up gut, all the while my heart was deepening and becoming more alive and attuned. My strong discomfort with such raw vulnerability revealed to me a protection so deep it wasn't even conscious, for I am not speaking of a superficial distaste for dependency (I am happy to ask for help when I need it) or an insistence on being self-reliant. This shudder of armor ran deep in the marrow of my being. I can well imagine dying without having known this shield, it was that subtle, hidden, and never appearing to be in the way of living life fully or loving well. And yet, here it was revealed, coming to awareness. It surprised me, and since it was such an intensely visceral sensation, it was clear to me that it needed attention, TLC, and integration. An unconscious part of me had been left out in the cold and needed to be seen and loved. Given an opening, life will always move in the service of true wholeness and unconditional love.

Wonder of wonders, how love works. It was so engaging to notice that even with what appeared to be a deeply embedded pattern, once consciousness shone its light, it was shiftable. What initially looked like a behavior set in concrete and unmovable, instead, loosened and relaxed.

Much to my surprise, I have by now both metaphorically and literally put my head on my friends' and family's laps.

CHAPTER FIVE

Unconditional love must include our precious human selves. I am often asked the same question when it comes to looking at our humanity, paying attention to how we are uniquely wired – the question usually has different flavors but it comes down to "why do that?" Why look at or show interest in our humanity, our personality? Especially when you have had a glimpse or more of your true nature and the bounty of living from an infinitely larger place which you know to be the truest reality.

Being awake is being viscerally aware of our connectedness, how everything is interconnected . . . not divided, not apart, not distanced from **anything**. Unconditional love means nothing is left out. It is intimate with every bit of life—10,000 things! Unconditional love, by its very name unconditional, is accepting and inclusive of ALL. Presence means being present to what is appearing each moment. No matter what is showing up. Doesn't that, therefore, also include our humanity, our personalities? As long as we are alive in this dimension, we are reliant on our human form to function, to carry on in everyday life.

Additionally, awareness, the very ground of being, the infinite, is expressed through form. Doesn't it make sense then that we are wired to be curious about and attentive to this expression? That we would wonder about our inner life, wonder what animates us, why we suffer, and are called to know ourselves, in a nonending deepening inquiry? Compassionate and deep self-inquiry has the potential of opening our minds, hearts and fists, allowing unconditional love, clarity and awareness to flow endlessly in and through us. The infusion of such love and clarity opens our eyes and ears to the inner world of "others", to a deepening kindness for all humanity and an understanding of our universal pain and suffering. It reveals our common source as well as opens us to be attuned and receptive to the essence of the animal kingdom, the make-up of the trees and the rivers and the flowers, all forms of our common source.

Typically, the question of "why would I look at myself," especially the painful parts, often comes from being concerned with inflating self-involvement or egotism, or placing undue value on what is real in the relative world but not the Absolute world (an unreal distinction since all is one). One of the biggest resistances to not fully facing our small selves is not wanting to hurt—understandably, we shy away from pain. And yet, paradoxically, when we genuinely pay attention and explore, beyond shame or judgment, how we are wired, self-involvement is dissolved. Within an honest and serious inquiry of our inner world—who am I—we open ourselves to the transcendent.

Our inner life is so much more than a personal thing. It can have a fundamental flavor to it. Know thyself so consciousness might expand, love deepen, courage grows, so reactivity can be understood and evaporate, projections withdrawn. What a gift to an ailing world! We only have to look around to see the chaos and divisiveness of the world we live in, where many have no idea who they are—as humans much less as Source. The world is crying out for kindness, for caring and understanding.

I don't think we can truly know ourselves, take good long looks within, care how we treat the people in our lives and all sentient beings, without loving ourselves. Accepting our humanity, opening our hearts, our minds, and our guts so we allow life to dissolve our unconscious shields, over and over again. Many of us have become accustomed to living with our guard up to some degree, to feeling unworthy in one regard or another, to seeing the surface of ourselves as the whole picture. It is in the inner delving, with kindness and compassion towards every part of our humanity, that we re-connect with our completeness and remember ourselves as we truly are—vast, eternal Love.

Vast, eternal Love asks everything of us, even (or especially) when it goes against the mind's desire for control, and it demands more than we can ever comprehend.

Love is not sappy nor nostalgic. It is not a desire nor a destination. It is not needy nor fearful. It is not lacking nor hungry. It is an energetic force of truth that will burn anything and everything in its way of being, bringing all life back to its beautiful and pure home.

Love enhances; it liberates and heals. It transforms our deepest beings, regardless of how our conditioned self feels about the transforming lessons.

It will melt your heart and be fiercely demanding all in one breath.

It is personal—seeing my grandsons' faces melts every bone in my body—and it is astonishingly impersonal. Love abides in and contains everything and everyone as a profound acceptance of whatever is happening. Love and truth are profoundly neutral.

I was taking a short walk between errands, having just enough energy to make my way through picking up two things I needed. Up ahead I became aware of a small group of people standing on the sidewalk, creating a horseshow around an elderly man who was struggling to get back on his feet. As I got closer, I saw the blood on his forehead and nose, realizing he had fallen. I wondered why the young people were not physically helping him up, but they were handing him Kleenex and handkerchiefs, which he declined politely since he had his own.

Everything in me wanted to extend my arm to him and walk him to wherever he was headed, knowing he was stunned and likely not steady on his feet.

And yet, I knew I did not have the energy to do that. I could not genuinely help him, so I walked on by, with a heavy heart. I had no choice but to face what was true—I was in no position to physically help this man.

CHAPTER SIX

DARKNESS OF THE UNKNOWN

If I had a preference, I would not have been sick and certainly not for that long without a known treatment. Being awake, a double-edged sword, means everything is felt and experienced, *and* Presence requires and allows *more* to be felt and experienced, without the stickiness of attachment and identification. There was something godly about being sick, something deeply beneficial about living in the dark long enough to find real peace inside the unknown. It was freeing to genuinely have no control over my circumstances—I might not "like" it, but I knew enough to ride the waves.

When my two oldest grandsons were little, they lived in a house that had a long cement walkway on one side. At night this "alley" was pitch-black. One evening, the three of us were tossing a soccer ball back and forth and one swift kick sent it careening down the dark corridor. As far as the boys were concerned this was the end of our playing with the ball. They were terrified of going into the dark. No offers of handholding, flashlights, or running in and out quickly screaming into the dark at the top of our lungs, could persuade them to step foot in the alley. The ball could only be retrieved in the daylight.

We are often afraid of the dark. We are afraid of what we do not know, and afraid of our psyche's unconscious, which lives in the dark and to varying degrees is unknown to us. Many of us are afraid of death (the ultimate unknown). If we are lucky, we also know the even deeper and stronger light that resides inside every sentient being. In my experience, living as pure harmony means growing up, maturing, and committing ourselves to kind and conscious awareness of our inner world—layer upon layer of not knowing. All arisings, personal or karmic, whatever their nature, can be kindling for burning. Embracing this allows the gestation to happen; finding a neutrality in growth (whether it is painful, ecstatic or incomprehensible) can be the portal that allows the dissolution into the very Light we are seeking and which is seeking us.

Knowing this profound reality allows us to stay present with whatever might arise—whatever is encountered—whatever is seeking to be known. There's a mysterious full circle hanging on our willingness to give everything . . . everything to Presence.

But God's own descent
Into flesh was meant

As a demonstration
That the supreme merit
Lay in risking spirit
In substantiation.
Robert Frost

I had a strong and kind medical team working with me. There is still no known "cure" for Long Covid and I had relied a great deal on homeopathy. The remedies had given me some relief, here and there, but the important thing for this book is what I noticed inside myself. I began to call myself Charlie Brown, after the cartoon character, who, no matter how many times Lucy grabs the football away from him at the last moment causing him to fall flat on his back, still attempts to kick the football every single time she tells him to.

I would find myself feeling better, almost, almost okay and would think "ahh, I am better now and can begin to recover," only to face a disappointing crash when I felt awful again a day or so later. No matter how many times this happened I seemed to have no control over this dynamic—even while watching and noticing how I was setting myself up each and every time. All I could do was to be fully present to it and hold it softly and lightly.

All I could do was be aware of it and live it out.

I mimicked Charlie Brown until I came to the end of my rope. Hanging onto hope was taking up so much energy, which was in short supply and leaving me wrung out. I only realized this in hindsight when

I came to see that I had actually lost hope. It had simply disappeared, was not operating anymore. I was living in a state of not knowing (will I recover? is this my new normal? might it get worse?) where I lived without hope. At the same time, I knew in my cells that I couldn't know how this would go and was living in a state I had not known before this moment. I spent a lot of time reflecting on what hope meant to me and watched what it was like to not have it to grab hold of when there was no physical relief from being sick and no ready answers from the medical world. I felt cold and adrift, not even alive as Long Covid moved through my entire system. This was a big deal—I had even written a book on resiliency! Throughout my earlier years hope had kept me sane; it had been the driving force for meaning and growth and expansion. And now, it had become clear that I had been unaware of a subtlety of hope—the subtlety the mind brings in of expecting a certain kind of outcome. An outcome of our choosing. There is a hook in how, for the most part, we humans experience and live with hope. We are assuming a desired and predictable conclusion.

Suddenly, in the snap of a finger, hope was gone.

Around this time, I had a second dream: It is a long dream laced with grounded ecstasy and faith.

The overall message or theme of the dream was that I was in a committed relationship with a beautiful, deeply wise and divine man, who was very modern in his looks, but in my bones I knew him to be Jesus.

The dream opens with me in a pool with a family member. I move to get out of the pool and there is an exchange in which my relative asks me to stay in the pool. Being asked to do something different from my own preference registers within me as a mere whisp of recognition, it doesn't propel me to do what she wants. Not unkindly I say I'd rather eat outside the pool.

I am now on the high ledge of the swimming pool. It is a long jump to the ground. I ask another family member for help in getting down and to take my hand, my waist, or somehow help me soften the jump. He shows me something I am wearing that has a tassel or some apparatus that I can use to make the jump. I hold onto it and am amazed at the gentle ease of the jump and landing.

The dream has now shifted to a scene with lots and lots of people on a very large boat which has sailed a vast ocean and is now docked. We are all going to get into a line to get off the boat and are moving through long, long corridors. Many new folks show up, getting in line. These folks are either immi-grants, or lacking wealth or class—they are visibly different from the people that are coming from other corridors. I make room for several of the wealthy to get in line before I begin to walk the line, ahead of the immigrants. I notice that my beloved is fur-ther back and in order to walk with him, or directly in front of him, I have to allow many more folks to walk ahead of me. I do just that. It brings to mind the biblical quote "the greatest amongst you shall be servants"—humility and service to truth above all else. I recently read that Krishnamurti always went to the back of the food line, allowing everyone else to get their food first. Reading that brought me to tears.

In the dream, we have arrived at a large square meeting hall or some such place. It is indoors. This is where something important will go on. I am in a white wedding gown and see my beloved reclining in the corner of a high-armed sofa, peacefully reclining and observing. In my gown, I playfully jump over him in order to cuddle closely next to him, cradling myself into the side of his body. I am in a grounded, blissful state (what was so moving was the feeling of such complete, quiet, unquestioned alrightness). He is my beloved, I am his—it is the most natural way there is. There is no doubt whatsoever.

As we lay there, I become aware that I deeply want to make love to him. I say out loud, "I want to make love with you"—in such a way that I know **how much** I want to be joined and physical with him. He doesn't say anything.

I say to him, "You could say something." I say this playfully, there is no awkwardness or insecurity between us.

He says, "Not yet".

And adds, "We are in New Orleans and the environment is influencing you."

I get the impression that he is telling me something for my own good. At the same time, he is aware of and letting me know there is some divine timing going on—for my own benefit. The truth of what he is saying (and the promise it implies) registers deeply within and I awaken from the dream.

There are "small" messages embedded in this dream. I have a voice; I am tethered to the mystery, and I am greatly aligned. I am at ease with "getting in line," humbly. My desire for an even profounder full unity is visible and unabashed.

The dream begins with a swimming pool and moves to the ocean. In Jungian symbology water typically represents the unconscious. And large bodies of water, like the ocean, can represent the collective unconscious, the home of the archetypes, one of which is the Self or Center that Jung ascribes as the experience of God in various religions.

Large bodies of water, representing the collective unconscious, also brings to mind the ignorance we live with collectively, the fact that all of us live with some level of unconsciousness and are all in this vast unknown together. We live within the collective mind, and, agreeing with Jung's long-ago observation, it appears that the unconscious mind is vaster than the conscious mind.

The unconscious is vast and often difficult to see into, similar to the depths of a large body of water. Staying with Jung, from his *Red Book*, "The ageless waters know everything; they have been present since the beginning and conserve everything in their liveliness—nothing is forgotten." Looking at it from this perspective, isn't it possible that delving

into the ageless waters of the unconscious can be illu-
minating and freeing—even as it requires us to be
courageous?

In the dream I start the journey in and out of
a pool—a smaller, contained body of water—appar-
ently pointing to some personal patterns that have
become conscious. The dream is pointing to a famil-
iarity with the personal unconscious; an ease that has
opened for me over the years and years of devotion to
knowing myself.

Moving to the ocean, I have the sense that the
dream is a portend of things to come. I am on a boat,
on the surface of the water; I am not swimming in the
ocean, and yet I become aware of and easily at home
with a very sweet sense of humility. To be aligned
with a Christ consciousness is being in a state of abiding and awesome surrender. It is serving truth; it is
an ease with reality and an ongoing flow with each
changing moment.

I consider Jesus my first teacher—long before I
had any idea of there being such a thing as a spiritual
teacher. Having been raised Jewish, Jesus was non-ex-
istent in my world—or perhaps more accurately said,
he was not allowed in my world. I don't remember
questioning that but when, in my early thirties, I was
introduced to him as a human man demonstrably living as a divine being in human form, I at first wondered if I was crossing some arbitrary and dangerous
line by my genuine and intuited pull towards him.

There had been nothing in my life up to that

point that would have indicated to me or to anyone else that I was looking for a recognition of divine consciousness. I had vague but definite, if certainly inexpressible, intuitions about there being more to life than what I had been experiencing, and I knew enough to hear the quiet, still voice within suggest I was looking for peace of mind and for what I called a personal relationship with God. Since these gleanings were private and not reflected deeply upon, I came to studying the teachings and life of Jesus innocently and freshly.

And . . . and . . . those many years ago, there had been *no* doubt I recognized Jesus immediately. I, again, intuited . . . in that deeply knowing place that leaves us with no question of its truth . . . I intuited that Jesus was revealing and expressing exactly what I could not have named within myself. It was a very quiet recognition; one that left me feeling guided, validated, and very much in awe. I could not have named it in that moment, but I had my first glimpse of what we are and my first remembering of what I realized I had always known.

In the dream I am in a wedding gown and completely at home with the divine consciousness that Jesus represents. I am aware of the call to an even profounder experience of oneness; the dream appears to be pointing to a deepening process that is moving on its own, suggesting I continue as is and allow Life to do its thing. I feel no resistance to being influenced by New Orleans. I take it as a matter of fact that I am being influenced by New Orleans. Why New Orleans still baffles me a bit. I resonate with its initials, NO, however. It has taken me a lifetime to truly know and live the cliché that *no* is a full sentence.

CHAPTER SEVEN

Shortly after this dream, the distress of losing hope began to evaporate. I was certainly being shown timing . . . Life's timing, not mine. As soon as it became clear—named—I had lost hope, had let go of the unconscious longing for a certain outcome, I felt better being conscious of what was happening. *The truth shall set you free*. The delicious irony is that illusory hope was taking up valuable real estate. Without its energy and desires, there was space and room for greater presence and the sweet current of love to overflow even more. Having more spaciousness allowed me to wonder even more deeply, what is the field beyond hope? It is not "no hope." How does faith enter the frame and how does doubt teach us? The circumstances had not changed and yet my heart and my being were often lighter.

Whether it be fear/anxiety or hope we are holding onto, we are distancing ourselves from the present moment. Misleading hope was keeping me, in subtle and not so subtle ways, looking to a certain belief about the future and distracting me, again in subtle and not so subtle ways, from the physical sensations in my body. Understandably! Most of us humans do not want to fully face reality. It is not for the faint of heart. It requires great devotion to looking for and knowing what is real, what is true, no matter how it feels. Our minds, designed for survival and feeling good, cannot grok this.

I didn't feel better physically, which continued to be quite rough at times, but I was more clearly grounded in the present moment reality of being sick instead of holding out for an imagined wellness. In the here and now of things (the field that is beyond **all** opposites) on any given day, I find myself feeling the pure sensation of pain in my gut. I sense the feeling of PTSD from the trauma of feeling unsafe in my body resurfacing. At the same time, I feel deep, deep love wash through me. My mind is foggy from the pain in one moment and clearer than ever in another moment. I feel pure jangled nerves radiating from my nervous system reacting to chronic pain as I gaze out my living room window aimlessly; or over the months, as I sit watching the world go by, not knowing what today or the next day will bring. I am more and more aware that this has always been the truth—we have no idea what this afternoon or next month might bring, and as I settle into this awareness I watch my heart's unending gratitude for being conscious. Amazingly, the whole universe is within us, and what a marvel for any of us to know this.

It makes such a difference. No matter the circumstances, it is possible to find our way into conscious, radical acceptance. Even when conscious, radical acceptance includes living in the pitch-black darkness of uncertainty and unknowing.

Life continued in much the same way. I continued to be sick—with periods of feeling better peppered in. I read articles and studies about Long Covid; friends sent me dozens of suggestions, my doctors tried to relieve my symptoms, and my life stayed narrow. I learned the hard way that exercise exacerbated Long Covid symptoms. As I walked half a block very, very slowly, with my hands held behind my back, I began to remind myself of my grandfather in his elderly years. I sorely missed all the foods I loved to eat which now upset my increasingly delicate digestive system. I missed mobility, longing for my favorite hikes and woods.

CHAPTER EIGHT

Almost two years into being sick I had a third dream. This dream came at the very beginning of a time I had decided to take time off, to unplug from everything and everyone. Over time, and interspersed with lots of rest, I had managed to do a few sessions with folks and see a friend or two on occasion. Now, I chose not to work, socialize, or be engaged. I wanted to see if that might help me feel better or inform how to feel better.

In the dream, I have been in a long-running play, with a large role. The play and the role have come to an end. It is a big deal since it has gone on for such a long time and a lot of strong bonds have been formed. I am aware of feeling great fondness and love for many of my co-players. It is noticeable to me that I only hug those with whom I have genuinely shared something real. (A shout-out to increasing authenticity!)

It is time to leave and say our final good-byes.

For some reason I have been gifted or left with two horses. As I look at them I notice they are bridled and strong work horses. I think about how to get them home and where to house them and realize it is better to leave them here overnight and consider what to do the next day.

It is worth pointing out here that the dream ended with me not yet knowing what I would do with the horses. Knowing it is possible to "continue" a dream in a waking state by entering the unconscious consciously, I allowed the dream to further unfold. What makes this process particularly powerful is the bypassing of thought and willfulness. As the dream continued in my waking state, it became obvious and clear that I needed to unbridle the horses and find them an open field to graze and roam or lie down as their natural drive dictated.

Upon reflecting on the dream, two things got my attention: the work horses, as well as the ending of something that had gone on for a long, long time, something I played a central role in. The role had gone on for so long it felt like all I had ever known. I knew something embedded and strongly habitual was coming to an end. The NO of New Orleans came back into view.

Like so many of us, my life had been completely run by my conditioned need for approval and love. This need of looking for approval and love every which way not only formed what appeared to be my entire personality, it also fully restricted any genuineness or recognition of how I truly felt, or what I naturally needed or wanted. Like so many of us I turned into a pretzel, bending myself to not upset anyone for fear of rejection and keeping myself very small. God forbid, I should disappoint someone by setting a boundary and saying no! It has been years since I have searched for love and approval to boost my sense of self. That search was no longer running my life or behavior. I had a sense the dream was pointing even deeper— more into the core instinct of egoic survival, which I will delve into further in a moment.

I thought about the larger body of water, the vast unconscious we all live within as one mind. My own piece of the collective unconscious, my own inheritance from generations of ancestry, is one of victimization and oppression. It hearkens back to the dream with Jesus where I need to consciously and generously make room for the immigrants (my collective lineage). It is in looking back upon this message that I have come to a dawning recognition of the generational layers of victimization and oppression I was born into—and as I watch the world grapple with the same issues of equality and representation I am aware of the enormity of the collective unconscious we all house, and how it feels to be restrained like those bridled work horses. Oppression and victimization are such profound bridling. When we feel oppressed and/ or victimized, for the most part, there often appears to be no room to say or act upon an empowered no.

I am not referring to a no that comes from our mind's resistance, nor a mind's desire for control but from the no that sets boundaries and reminds us where true power lives. In our deepest beings we have assistance, we are aligned, we are expansive and love is limitless.

It is very meaningful for me to have become aware of such an integral part of how I unconsciously identified and know that it is time to let it all go. Letting go of something ancient and entangling can alter how you relate to yourself, friends and family, the collective, and the environment. It moves the energy from this is being done *to* me into this is being done *for* me. Not putting out any trails of victimization and/or oppression means there is nothing to catch onto; it can literally change the dynamics of relating.

The dream affirmed something old was ending and something new readying to be on its way.

While I don't have any personal associations with horses I can relate to them as beautiful forces of the energy of life. The instinctual and natural way life expresses itself in form.

In the dream the beautifully natural and instinctive life force had its expression reigned in. This is a very clear view of how our conditioning drives us. Being disconnected from my natural, instinctive life force had robbed me of freedom, authenticity, and the strength to know and express my truth.

Horses can represent this authenticity—an authenticity and truth-saying that is often shaken by trauma. The horse is majestic and attuned; they are often used to help people heal from trauma. Jung saw the horse archetype, in its natural and unbridled state, as symbolic of our courageous and empathic capacities, representing our potential strength of power and vulnerability.

I knew this was an "inside" job. The bridled work horses had been fully embedded in my cells throughout my life. There was something powerful showing up for me, as if I had reached directly into the very core of my human life as it had played out. To me these bridled work horses represent the survival instinct that is built into our humanity—the survival instinct built into the "laws" of this earthly existence for every living being. The instinct to remain tethered to everything we are taught we need in order to live according to our world's values and yardsticks. The instinct our mind relies upon for its relevance and for its vitality. The instinct that often pools in our gut (second brain) and will clench at the merest whiff of perceived danger.

Living beyond our mind's clutch to its survival is stepping aside so Life itself freely flows through the Being, as Life itself moves and guides every step and as Life itself runs the show. Our personal "role" takes a step back, trusting a bigger picture and a mystery we cannot fathom. It is a dance of not being identified or attached to the conditioned mind; to the degree we are attached or identified is the degree to which we will suffer. While this is not bad or wrong; it is an invitation to go inside and with an open heart explore what is calling you to itself. Moving beyond what is tying you to egoic survival is a dance of harmonious alignment between our cherished humanity and the supreme Divine. It is a dance of contemplation, truth-saying, kind authenticity, and radical acceptance.

As if the horses were speaking to me, I knew to free them from their put-upon burdens and give them endless pastures to roam and delight in their release.

I automatically knew this dream was pointing to something important. And I instinctively knew there was more to this dream and my previous dreams than met the eye or any apparent superficiality. I decided to paint two magnificent horses lying in a pasture, relaxed, at ease and surrounded by the greens of the grass and leaves on a large tree, under a peaceful sky. In fact, I painted the two previous dreams as well— the vivid yellow daffodils set against a gray world and a full-of-depth portrait of the man of my dreams I called Jesus.

The small quiet voice within, will point the way towards what is needed. It behooves us to listen, always.

CHAPTER NINE

Around this time, I arranged a spiritual healing for myself. Once again, intuition led me to a gifted healer, Debra Martin. Debra, an Intuitive Healer, worked with spirit guides, angels, and the Divine. Going beyond our six senses, into a world of invisible sensations, imaginations and intuition can and often does conjure up a judgment of flakey or woo-woo. While there certainly are charlatans and questionable people and modalities in the psychic world, my experience, when there is a genuine alignment, is a sense of a very real experience. I know something real has taken place when a visible shift has taken place. When some pain or struggle has left the scene, shifted the energy and there is genuine peace and fresh air throughout my entire system.

I went into this healing with the same attitude I had for every other healing modality I tried— having no idea if it would make any difference at all but feeling pulled to try. I seemed to walk that fine line between not expecting anything and willing to see if something might just help.

It was a powerful healing—powerful on a physical level, feeling my body respond to the treatment and even more powerful spiritually.

On the physical level I was aware of many sensations: pressure at the top of my head and then an immediate pressure in my throat as if some expression was waiting.

The rest of the session concentrated on my belly and esophagus.

Near the end of the session, I can hear the instruction of *let go. Let it all go.* All that I have held can be let go. Let go of the clench, let go of holding on (for dear life). I appear to be in the belly of the whale—the seat of survival—our human impulse to struggle and not die. It brings to mind the ending of the survival machinery I played out in the previous dream. This feels like a further reminder as well as a manifestation.

I have a slight sense of beings around me—giving me an opportunity to say thank you. Thank you for being with me today and thank you for helping me heal. My maternal grandmother is "standing" next to me rubbing my leg, comforting me. It was this grandmother who made it clear to my mother not to go through aborting me, as she had been pressured to do. I am aware that without my grandmother stepping in, I might not be here.

And most surprising, my father shows up, young and healthy, walking towards me, with his arms opened wide for a hug. I am aware of my response, both shocking and as natural as the sun rising and setting. I rejoice as I move into his arms and return the hug. At some point, it becomes very clear to me that we met spirit to spirit in this moment and the human sexual and physical abuse on his end and the hatred and terror on mine was not at all . . . not in the least . . . present or even alive in that profound moment.

I knew enough not to try making any sense of this or try to understand it. The entire interaction felt entirely joyful.

Several months after this healing I found out my father had attempted to molest a friend, when she and I were around sixteen or seventeen. I found myself furious that he had dared try to hurt someone outside our family. I was bereft that she had to experience the sickness in my family. It brought me to a clearer view of my father's warped and troubled mind. It became clear to me that some unconscious part of me had often doubted the abuse, and hearing from my friend pushed me to a reckoning I hadn't known I needed. I was oddly reassured by the truth of that.

As if on cue, my father "appeared" to me a few nights later and, in a sincerely remorseful way, told me he was sorry, so very sorry. I melted.

I felt something even more relevant happened here—any ties between us (including from his end) were untied, unknotted and we were both free from what had been enacted between us. He was freed from remorse, and I was freed from oppression.

I found myself weeping and weeping. So much more went on than I had any idea about.

As I look back upon this healing, what holds my attention the most is the moment that I become aware that Life/God/Spirit is whispering in my ear. I hear a distinct request: "Promise me . . . give me your word . . ."

I am aware of not knowing what is being asked of me and, even more importantly, I am clear the answer cannot come from my head. I need to sit with this, let it simmer in its own sauce and timing and wait until, in my heart, I know what promise is being prompted.

One day, it becomes clear to me. Source, the energy that animates all of life, is asking me to trust Life. Trusting at the human level and trusting at the Absolute level are two very different things. Trusting at the human level is often filled with legitimate challenges. Who has not, over a lifetime, experienced betrayal, disappointment and, in some cases, cruelty. Who has not been let down by promises, unfulfilled dreams, and unrequited love. We make our way through relationships, work, and play, finding some level of trust that allows us to keep going. To try our hand at love and happiness again and again.

Trust Life. It is clear to me that feeling forsaken at various times during this illness is revealing not only a lack in trust but an unconscious belief that God is only in the light of things, not in the darkness or scary unknown.

I am reminded of the prayer I have lived with—may "I" know peace no matter the circumstances—that it is possible to know, truly and cellularly know, that in the darkest of nights Life is good and no one is alone, ever. Forsaken is a feeling; it is an understandable reaction to a perception of feeling forgotten, being in the desert for forty days, alone with our demons and losing sight or feeling of our deepest all-right-ness. It is an invitation to trust more deeply, viscerally, when living in the darkness, without knowing, allowing trust to build and call out to us.

In the days and weeks following the healing I find myself exhausted. The healing itself feels huge. It also feels like there is a surge of energy in me that has yet to be fully felt.

I do not feel better, physically, for weeks and weeks after the healing. I grieve like I have never grieved before. Some dam is breaking; a heartbreak for our entire humanity, all the pain and torment we have experienced from the beginning of our time here on earth and for the millions of ways we hurt each other and miss out on the very connection we yearn and long for. For the darkness we create through our actions and for the forgetting of what we truly are.

As energy moves through me, I become aware of my heart exploding open.

In some deep way I begin to feel better. I feel more aligned with my whole self again. I feel the beginning of genuine healing. I feel the wholeness that has been eclipsed by fear and anxiety.

I feel an inner strength that I have not felt since being sick. It feels essential.

I have come to see this integration as a new and enormous trust in Life. No matter how much we intellectually understand that living an awake life is one of being at peace with all there is, in order to truly integrate our humanity with the infinite, we are faced with knowing and loving every single part of ourselves, including aspects we shudder and cringe at the mere idea of. Trust Life? As I mentioned above, given our common human experience of betrayals and hurt between each other, this can be a tall order.

Intuiting this new fledgling of trust, I offer a prayer. I offer a complete opening of my gut—an offer of faith—an offer of an unclenched gut. Here am I.

Early the next morning I have a dream. I am getting married. There is much happening in the way of preparation—everyone in my family and many others as well have congregated and are sitting in chairs, filling the room where the wedding will take place. The room itself is indoors and contained. It appears I am marrying my ex-husband—or at least I assume so since he is there, also busy getting things and himself ready for the occasion.

I then realize that the woman who is officiating has gone into another room and is occupied doing something there while waiting for us to be ready for her.

I send someone to tell her we are ready and she can come back into the room and begin things.

I wake up.

The next part of the dream occurs while I am semi-awake and on the edges of falling back to sleep.

I am marrying God. We are outdoors, in the middle of an exquisite, vast and boundless field, and, except for the officiant, there is no one else there. I am barefoot, with a beautiful crown of flowers on my head. A long gray braid trails down my back. I am dressed fully in white in a draped fabric that is completely off my shoulders, tied at the waist with rope and ankle length (hearkening to biblical times.)

God is in outline . . . amorphous. His outline is in the shape of an oval. Ovals often symbolize unity; beyond any angular lines it is a resonant shape that blends circular ends into an integrated form, transcending duality. The God figure is outlined above his head to below his toes in iridescent white, except for His hands. They are made of flesh and blood and are holding my hands. In the cradle our hands have formed lies a bouquet of blood red roses interspersed with white daisies. It reminds me of love that has more deeply fused with itself (blood kin), combined with the purity of innocence, the freshness of living each moment brand new.

I turn towards God and, without any volition on my part, slowly glide inside him, until I am completely embedded within Him. Witnessing this I can see the whisps of the full "me" and the fullness of God.

The woman officiant is facing us. She speaks for a bit and then pronounces us ONE.

I have longed for a dream of holy union for longer than I can recall and this dream filled my heart to overflowing. My heart's desire wholly aligned with Reality.

CHAPTER TEN

Decades and decades ago, I went to Dachau—the site of a concentration camp outside of Munich. I was traveling through Germany with a friend and we decided to walk through the camp. I was unprepared for what it would feel like; being, at that time of my life, unconscious to a great deal of the darkness in my own psyche, let alone the profound impact the collective darkness unleashes into our atmosphere.

I remember wanting to go because I had read about the small chapel the Carmelite nuns had built in the center of the camp.

I entered the gates of Dachau and was immediately thrown off my heels. Years later when visiting Hiroshima I would have the same experience, but at that moment I had never known or felt such physical, dense, dark, and sinister energy. I began weeping uncontrollably, as I felt the ground, the buildings, the barbed wire fencing, and the sheer immensity of ground the camp covered all oozing a black darkness.

I don't know if I literally fell to my knees but the feeling was one of not being able to move through the physical energy.

We found our way to the chapel. It is a small, whitewashed building. My recollection is a bell outside the chapel that has been ringing non-stop since the nuns built the chapel. The inside of the modest building houses a lovely altar, several pews of seating and many, many lit candles. If memory serves me correctly, the nuns have kept the candles lit since the moment the building was completed. The entire structure is modest in size and scale.

And yet, after sitting for a short time, the sense of light, the power of silence, and the felt-sense of well-being was literally palpable. The simplicity, beauty, and magnitude of the light and silence wove their way into every fiber of my being.

Walking back through the camp, I was completely at ease and, truth be known, did not even register the darkness of the camp at all.

It has been said we are souls having a human experience. That we are spirits here, on this earthly dimension of separation and opposites, learning how to love. What does it mean to experience . . . to know in our bones that we are the field of love, of truth, beyond any opposites? Since we humans have been alive on this planet we have lived with duality; it is a planet of duality and we have perpetrated and felt the weight of darkness and ignorance. The time we are living in now is no exception to that reality.

And yet . . . what truly is darkness? It is also said we humans cannot know **full** reality, the **full** dimension of God. As with the tree that grows into the soil through feel, it is something we can intuit, instinctively sense and feel, but most often love, true love. . . truth and not illusion calls us . . . to *feel* the darkness that is hidden, misunderstood. While it appears very dark when truly experienced it opens into a lavishness of light.

We are asked over and over again, what is our fruitful and useful response to so much darkness?

CHAPTER ELEVEN

At the time of the spiritual healing, when my father showed up, I had a reflexive thought: I am glad it is not my mother who is here.

This got my attention. At some point in the healing, the facilitator mentioned feeling someone giving her a butterfly kiss on the cheek.

Sitting with the kiss, it dawned on me, sometime later, that my mother had gently and unobtrusively kissed me through the facilitator. I was grateful that it was a small step forward; one I could go towards and not be overcome.

One night as I'm lying quietly, unbidden, my mother "comes" to me. If you remember that all consciousness is energy, just as we take on this energy in the human form, I imagine our deceased family members' energetic presence can be sensed, felt or possibly even seen and heard. While being visited by people no longer alive on this planet remains quite mysterious to me, once again, I am fully aware of how real the experience is and how profound the effect can be.

She wants me to know that she loved me; she felt pressured to abort her pregnancy and was relieved when she didn't go through with it. She also lets me know that she tried, many times, to intervene between my father and myself, but was unable. She wanted me to know how sorry she was.

I was moved to tears, but as the days went by I felt a resistance to her saying she had loved me. It did not ring true to my experience.

A couple of nights later I spontaneously remembered being around five or six years old, sitting on the edge of my mother's bed crying in pain with a yeast infection. My mother was sitting beside me with her arm over my shoulder, pulling me close into her.

I have remembered this scene many times over my lifetime and always rejected her care, assuming it was coming from guilt.

This evening, though, the energy palpably and instinctively shifted inside me, and I could feel the comfort in her embrace. Shock and relief went through me like electricity. I leaned further and further into the comfort and realized this was all I had needed. Instead of rejecting her care, I could let it in and something deep within could relax—deeply rest.

Several days later, I imagined myself sitting at the ocean's edge, head thrown back to meet the sun, while the waves, moving with the tide, covered my legs and waist. I stood up, turned around, and began to joyfully dance.

My mother loved, loved to dance. I have danced perhaps three times in my life.

Walking on my city block, one day later, I found myself smiling broadly and turned my eyes to the sky and said: "Mom, come dance with me. It is time we danced."

From that day forward I have felt a fondness for my mother that I literally have never felt. The deeply buried, unconscious, and subtle resentment I have carried is gone. I look inside (now that I know where to look) and feel around for the sticky places and feel only clean and clear air. I have a smile in my heart for my mother and I am in awe how life works its magic.

I intuit a link . . . a connection . . . amongst healing, awakening, and transcendence. I probably could make some reasonable explanation for this, but, instead, I am left in wonder and enormous gratitude. Some deep knowing inside delivers, through my dream, that my conscious intent and perception of being married to God is the truth. At the same time, through deep contemplation and healing I am at peace with my father and my mother. Is this a coincidence? Does it even matter? The freedom it delivers is awesome.

Love, true love . . . truth and not illusion calls us to see the darkness that is often hidden and appears very dark; open-ended and without any concepts or form. To repeat what I wrote above, it calls us into feeling what we cannot grasp . . . cannot comprehend. We are reminded that we can more easily feel this *mystery* than see it. It can be experienced but not grasped.

Our minds want to take hold of it, make it comprehensible and manageable, which, if we are lucky, we ultimately learn is a fool's errand. The fact that our mind cannot apprehend this is one of the reasons it often seems completely hidden and totally dark each time we look more deeply.

Living in the dark, experiencing being nowhere, a state that felt totally forsaken, miraculously transformed a deeply buried portion of my soul, my perspective and my capacity for love. Contemplation, introspection and presence of some deeper regions of my psyche changed my inner landscape.

Living in the unknown, patiently waiting on the truth that sets us free, is rewarded with the comfort of spiritual growth . . . with peace that knows there is **always** unknowing.

Trust is built through the patient waiting, no matter how long the wait. Trust is built through love suddenly showing up, independent of anything we might have done the moment preceding its arrival, filling us with greater joy and a greater devotion to do whatever work is required, no matter how strong the sorrow or anguish. Trust is built through experiencing and continuing to listen for that small quiet voice reminding us that we are not alone.

I say to all of us dedicated to a spiritual knowing, examine your life. Pay careful attention to the way you live out your calling. With all you heart, be thankful for your gifts, for your fumbles, for your assistances, for your shadow, for your largesse; and love and truth will help you stand strong in the face of subtle and overt attacks from within and without, as you continue to reflect, contemplate and deepen. Become comfortable with the uncomfortable!

This mystical, sacred union that declared itself in my dream—I am—reveals what we **all** really are, in essence. This holy marriage reveals our true nature of completion, being bound together as one heart and mind; this embodiment of pure love, is baked into our very being. The divine force and energy that animates every living thing on earth is a sacred law: to move us through personal and collective evolution and growth to transcend our humanity, by fully embracing our humanity. By moving beyond our mind's limitations we remember our true home and our true being.

The greatest gift we can give to ourselves is love. A love of God—a love of Self and self.

The God I speak of, the source of all energy of all of life, this ineffable is beyond words, beyond description. And yet, nothing is more real than the embodied realization of the love we truly are; that sweet, current of indefinable well-being that underlies and saturates every aspect of our humanness, even if we go about our business unaware of its being. To know inner peace, to taste this joy, to be the presence that is radiating light and love, is to be in full wonder and grace. It is knowing, in every cell of our beings that we are living on sacred ground; that all life is precious and all our hearts are beating as one.

EPILOGUE

Three years ago today, January 3, 2022, I contracted Covid with Long Covid following close upon its heels.

I continue to have periodic crashes. I have more and more periods of feeling healthy and energetic and even vibrant but, so far, I have not found a balance between too much and just enough activity. The post exercise malaise that is a hallmark symptom of Long Covid (the smallest amount of physical exertion can lead to days and days of debilitating crashes) is not as acute as it has been, but I am still subject to not knowing how my body will react to being active. I only know I have done too much when I crash—that depleted experience of having very little energy or at times none at all, which, in turn, will upset my messed up gut. So far, I have not been able to discern ahead of time, even as I stay closely attuned to my body during the activities.

The miracle of this long siege is not that I am completely and fully well. I continue to live not knowing what the next day will bring. It has always been that way; it is through grace that this knowing is more conscious.

The miracle is I am no longer afraid of being sick. The miracle is having the capacity to be present throughout the illness. The miracle is a slow draining away of a cellular anxiety I have lived with my entire life. The miracle is no longer experiencing my body as unsafe. The miracle is paying close attention to my body, knowing, truly knowing, how to care for my body; embodied and not dissociated. The miracle is being willing to get help when I feel uncompromisingly vulnerable.

Marriage vows include . . . in sickness and in health. How fitting!

I bow to the power of love and the power of the eternal and spacious present. I bow to our human capacity to withstand the power of unconditional love.

POETRY CITATIONS

"Setting Forth Together" in: *Just Begin Again – For the First Time* by Meister Eckhart. Lines 6-10.

Forty Rules of Love of Shams of Tabriz 1185-1248. Rule 29, lines 4-5.

"The Gift Outright" (in honor of John F. Kennedy's inauguration) in: *In the Clearing* by Robert Frost. Lines 1-6.

ACKNOWLEDGMENTS

Writing is a solitary process. But it takes a village to birth what has been written in one's heart.

I am grateful to Epigraph Publishing for doing the work it does – bringing spiritual wisdom into the world, for anyone and everyone who is aligned with something greater than themselves to pick up and read about others living that path.

Paul Cohen contributes that gift through his vision and his dedication to publishing. Thank you, Paul.

Sandra Capellaro edited the book as if it were her own. She fine-tuned it into a lovely harmony and was able to make it sing more clearly and seamlessly. That she and I found a kinship was an extra gift . . . one I did not take for granted.

Thank you Colin Rolfe for your steady eye and perspective in creating a beautifully designed book and for your support and care framing my words into an alive painting.

My village people, my dear, dear friends . . . Dona Tversky, Nancy Beckman, Hilary Foster, Christney McGlashen, Bill McGlashen, Teresa McGlashen,

Maddie DuFault . . . in ways known and unknown to them, kept me afloat and, between bringing me food and spiritual support, made it possible to write this book, even though I wasn't physically well.

I am grateful to Dorothy Hunt, Suzanne Marie, Dona Tversky and John Prendergast for honoring me by reading the manuscript, offering so many useful words of wisdom that helped the first draft grow into a clearer and more refined final version . . . and taking the time to lovingly write out their reflections on the book for a public blurb. It was all an act of love.

Thank you to my dear friend Jan Frazier, from the bottom of my heart. It means so much to me to have you accompany this book with your foreword and to join with me in reaching out to all the readers who are asking big questions and wanting to know life and reality more deeply.

My family is my rock. My sons, Craig and Rick; my daughter's-in-law, Eva and Julie and my soulful grandsons, David (and his wife Eleni), Daniel (and his girlfriend, Kavya), Joshua, Casey and Ryan, grace me with their trust. Our ongoing conversations are rich and I wouldn't miss our mutual love and our interactions for the world.

My son Rick generously read an early draft . . . sent me articles and videos to help the manuscript breath and open more widely. His unwavering support helped my spirit soar while my body fell apart.

I am blown away that my grandson, who is up to his eyebrows in art school, was willing and able to take the time to design and create the front and back cover of the book. I gave him a summary of the content and, from where I stand, he got it "just right". Thank you, Ryan.

ABOUT THE AUTHOR

Beth Miller has been practicing psychology for over 30 years. She had a long-standing private practice and taught at the University of San Francisco Medical Center, Stanford University, and California Institute of Integral Studies. For 25 years she gave seminars, talks and workshops on cultivating resilience.

After retiring she continued working with people who are ready to embody the open-ended discoveries of their true nature with their humanity. Knowing psychology and the visceral reality of our true nature allows her to help folks unknot their conditioning and live inside a greater consciousness. It is through deep acceptance, non-judgmental, open-hearted spaciousness and compassion that people remember their wholeness, remember their true home.

Her background in studying resilience – why some appear innately resilient and others are crushed by life – set the stage for the bigger question: what allows us to unconditionally love, no matter the circumstances of our lives?

The question, ultimately, opened her to a profound shift in consciousness . . . awareness of our true nature of pure Presence. Over the years this shift has become more and more embodied, a marvel in and of itself. A marvel to be consciously alive and present to life as it is.

www.ingramcontent.com/pod-product-compliance
Lightning Source LLC
Chambersburg PA
CBHW022036090426

42741CB00007B/1090